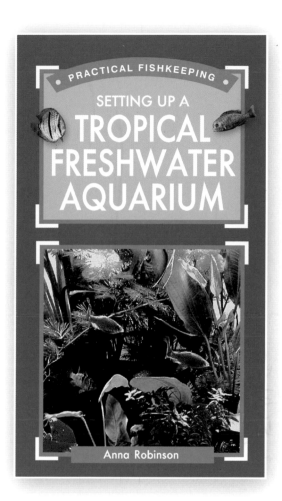

PRACTICAL FISHKEEPING

SETTING UP A
TROPICAL FRESHWATER AQUARIUM

Anna Robinson

Anna Robinson

D1393965

ABOUT THE AUTHOR

After keeping fish for many years as a child, Anna Robinson began working professionally in the aquarium industry at the age of 17. Since then she has gained a wide range of experience in all aspects of the hobby, particularly in dealing with queries from the fishkeeping community.

SCIENTIFIC CONSULTANT: Dr. Peter Burgess BSc, MSc, MPhil, PhD is an experienced aquarium hobbyist and international consultant on ornamental fish.

Commercial products shown in this book are for illustrative purposes only and are not necessarily endorsed by the author.

Photography: *Dr. Peter Burgess (p.27, p.38), Keith Allison, and courtesy of Tetra UK.*
Picture editor: *Claire Horton-Bussey*
Design: *Rob Benson*

Published by Ringpress Books, a division of Interpet Publishing, Vincent Lane, Dorking, Surrey, RH4 3YX, UK
Tel: 01306 873822   Fax: 01306 876712
email: sales@interpet.co.uk

First published 2002
© 2002 Ringpress Books. All rights reserved

No part of this book may be reproduced or transmitted in any form or by any means, electronic or mechanical, including photocopying, recording, or by any information storage and retrieval system, without permission in writing from the publisher.

ISBN 1 86054 245 X

Printed and bound in Hong Kong through Printworks International Ltd.

10 9 8 7 6 5 4 3 2 1

CAVAN COUNTY LIBRARY
ACC No. C/147412
CLASS NO. 639.34
INVOICE NO. 564 Cg
PRICE €4.79

CONTENTS

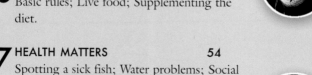

CHAPTER
1

PLANNING AN AQUARIUM

You have decided to buy an aquarium, but where do you start? Firstly, you should find a good aquatic shop (rather than a general pet shop), where there are staff who specialise in looking after fish.

The best way to find a trustworthy shop is through the recommendation of an aquarist friend, but if you don't know any other fishkeepers, you will have to find a shop yourself. Try local telephone directories or the area-by-area listings in fishkeeping magazines.

The first step to establishing a successful aquarium is to find a well-stocked aquatic shop, with knowledgable staff.

SHOP AROUND

Before you buy anything, have a look around the shops in your local area. Are the fish tanks clean? Are there dead or dying fish in them? Do they quarantine their fish before sale? Dip into the chapters in this book on feeding or water quality, and discreetly test the staff's knowledge with a few questions.

Don't necessarily settle for the closest shop to your home, but equally don't go right out of the district – ideally, you need a shop that has the same tap-water supply as yourself, and where the fish don't have to travel too far to reach your home aquarium.

You'll find a vast list of shops in *Practical Fishkeeping* magazine.

SIZE WISE

Buy the biggest aquarium your house and pocket can accommodate (within reason!). Larger volumes of water offer more stable temperatures and water chemistry, and compatibility problems between inhabitants are much less likely when the fish can get a reasonable distance away from each other. Aquariums of less than 10 gallons (45 litres) will make life harder for you. Perhaps just as importantly, you'll probably see many more fish that you like than you can fit into a small aquarium.

Large aquariums promote stability of water chemistry and temperature, so choose the biggest tank you can afford.

An hexagonal aquarium allows the fish plenty of room to swim around the tank.

Tall, narrow tanks should be avoided as surface area is limited.

THE RIGHT SHAPE

Think about shape. There should be plenty of surface area per volume of water as oxygen exchange occurs at the surface, so tall and narrow tanks are less practical. Also remember that with any tank deeper than about 55 cms (22 ins) it will be difficult to reach the bottom for planting or cleaning.

Consider also the materials used. Although acrylic or plastic aquariums can be much less heavy than glass tanks, they will scratch more easily, making them harder to keep clean.

KIT AQUARIUMS

Most aquariums come as complete 'kits', with all the equipment built in. This makes them neater and easier to set up, but check what they contain before buying.

LIGHTING

Kit aquariums usually have either one or two
fluorescent lights – go for two, if you can, as your tank
will look brighter and you'll be able to keep a wider
range of aquatic plants. Reflectors are a bonus as they
increase the amount of light reaching the aquarium.

HEATING

Tropical set-ups will have a heater-thermostat, to
maintain water temperature; ideally this should be out
of the fishes' reach (for example, in the filter
compartment), as fish have been known to smash them
or burn themselves on them. You will also need an
aquarium thermometer in order to check the
temperature. Internal glass thermometers are more
accurate than the stick-on type.

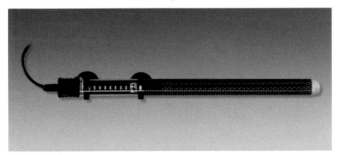

A heater-thermostat maintains water temperature.

FILTRATION

By far the most important piece of equipment in your
kit is the filter. Kit aquarium filters vary. Filtration is
covered in Chapter Three and the general types are
described here. In order to choose an adequate filter to
start off with, you will need to understand the main
filter functions:

Filtration is essential to the fishes' general health and well-being.

- Filters create water movement, usually by rippling the surface, in order to provide oxygen for the fish.
- They collect solid waste matter ('mechanical filtration') such as fish excrement and detached plant leaves, to keep the water clear.
- If they contain carbon (as many do, apart from undergravel filters), this carbon removes chemical pollution ('chemical filtration'), such as fish medications, and the yellow colour released by ornamental wood.
- 'Friendly' bacteria build up over the surface area of the filter material. These bacteria break down organic pollution (digestive waste matter from the inhabitants) and thus enable the fish to survive in the aquarium. (See Chapter Three for more details.) This is known as 'biological filtration', and is by far the most important function. Keep this in mind when looking at filters.

TYPES OF FILTER

UNDERGRAVEL FILTERS

The traditional and still widely-used filter. Undergravels consist of a plastic plate on the bottom

Pictured: Components of an undergravel filter prior to assembly.

of the tank, underneath the gravel, with a vertical tube attached to the plate, sticking up to just beneath the water surface. This is then powered by an air pump, or, less usually, by a powerhead (a water pump). By these means, water is pulled through the gravel and returned via the tube, the gravel itself becoming the filter.

DISADVANTAGES
- Undergravels are more awkward to clean, requiring regular 'hoovering' of the gravel to remove solid dirt.
- If powered by an air pump, they can also be a little noisy with a 'hum' from the pump and the sound of the bubbling. This does not happen with a powerhead.
- Undergravels make plant growth more difficult, due to high oxygen levels and the constant flow of water through the gravel bed.

ADVANTAGES
- Undergravels are cheaper than most other filters.
- They provide very stable biological filtration, and can cope with a heavy load of fish waste for their size, making them still the first choice of many fishkeepers.

INTERNAL FILTERS

There are many types of internal filter, but they generally consist of a box or container powered by a water pump, located inside the aquarium. The pump pulls water through a compartment (or compartments) in the box, usually containing sponge, carbon, ceramic rings, or a mixture of these. These filters can be very good or very bad, depending on the design. Most importantly, they must consist of several compartments or stages, so that not all the filter material needs to be washed at any one time; this is vital in order to preserve plenty of friendly bacteria.

Internal filters should be as large as possible in relation to the size of the aquarium.

Secondly, they should be as large as possible (within reason) for the size of the aquarium they serve. Some manufacturers advertise high filter output rates, but these in no way compensate for small filter volume. Many kit aquariums have a fairly unobtrusive compartment built into the back or a corner, containing a multi-stage internal filter plus room for the heater-thermostat.

DISADVANTAGES
- If internal filters consist of a single large sponge they can provide very unstable water conditions, due to the washing away of all bacteria every time the sponge is cleaned. Don't buy a filter of this type, or, if you have to, then buy two (or cut the sponge in half) so that you can clean them alternately.
- To cope with a reasonable amount of fish, they can be bulky, and, being inside the tank, are visible.

ADVANTAGES
- Easy to maintain (usually rinsing or replacing a piece of sponge in tankwater, not under the tap).
- They are silent.
- Growing plants is easier.

EXTERNAL FILTERS

These usually consist of a large canister topped by a water pump, situated below the aquarium and linked to it by pipes. Water drains from the aquarium, passes through the filter material in the canister, and is then pumped back up the pipe to the aquarium.

In the United States, smaller external filters that are attached to the back of the aquarium are common; these are much less popular in Britain.

DISADVANTAGES
- External filters are usually the most expensive option.
- They are large, and must be accommodated below the tank.
- The use of pipe-work creates plenty of opportunities for leaks and airlocks, especially when removing the filter for cleaning.

ADVANTAGES
- Although tricky to clean, because of their large size, external filters do not have to be cleaned so frequently.
- No unsightly equipment in the tank – there is virtually nothing visible in the aquarium.
- They are silent.
- Growing plants is easier.
- The fishkeeper can use any type of filter material in the canister that he or she might want.

External filter: for ease of photography, the filter is shown here next to the aquarium (and not below it, as normally advised).

As a first-time aquarist you will probably do best choosing a large, multi-stage internal filter, or a good undergravel filter. As filters vary so much in their design and maintenance, get as much information as you can on how to set-up and look after it at the time of purchase.

CHOOSING THE SUBSTRATE

Aquariums can have anything from fine sand to coarse gravel as their substrate. If using an undergravel filter, a medium pea-size gravel is best (around 5 mms/0.2 in particle size), but never use sand. For other types of filtration, provided that the gravel is rounded and not sharp, it is largely up to the aquarist.

A natural-coloured substrate makes fish feel more secure.

Finer substrates, such as sand, are easier on the fishes' mouths and on plant roots, but have a tendency to 'pack down' and stagnate more easily – they must be regularly stirred and/or hoovered to prevent this.

Most fishkeepers opt for a compromise grain size of between 2 mms and 6 mms (0.08-0.24 in). It is advisable to buy proper aquarium gravel; there are many coloured and natural types available, but darker substrates (rather than very garish or light-coloured ones) will make the fish feel more secure.

Rocks and ornaments provide much-needed hiding places for the fish.

DECORATING THE TANK

You can buy decorations such as rocks, ornaments and plastic plants at the same time as the aquarium, although real plants have to be left until the water has warmed up.

It is very important to decorate the tank. Ironically, as fish live in constant fear of predation, the more cover you provide, the more you will see of them. When fish know they have somewhere to go should danger threaten, they will be much happier about coming out into open water.

Plastic plants, rocks and purpose-made aquarium ornaments from your aquatic shop are obviously safe to use, but exercise care if collecting wood or rocks yourself. Some may have an adverse effect on the water, or you could accidentally introduce unwanted visitors, such as leeches or other parasites.

Fish will swim between areas of cover, so if you provide a well-decorated tank, you will see more of the inhabitants.

ROCKS

Buy rocks that are:
- Hard and inert (metamorphic rocks, such as granite or slate).

Avoid rocks that are:
- Sharp
- Crumbly or chalky
- Have small holes or cracks where fish may become stuck
- Have rusty or metallic veins running through them.

'Safe' wood can be bought from aquatic shops and makes an attractive addition to most tanks.

WOOD

Another popular ornament is wood that has lain in the ground or in peat bogs, where it has hardened and has taken on the appearance of drift wood. This is available from aquatic shops, looks very natural and can be very beneficial for some types of fish to chew on. However, it usually releases a brown colour (and sometimes tannic acid) into the aquarium water. If you dislike this discoloration, fresh activated carbon in your filter will remove it. Alternatively, you can soak the wood in a clean bucket of water, although it may take many weeks to remove all the colour.

BACKGROUND

Most fishkeepers also place something on the back of the aquarium to stop the wallpaper showing through. You can buy either stick-on underwater scenes, plain colours such as blue or black, or, more expensively, resin 'rock faces' that are affixed inside the tank with aquarium glue – give these 48 hours to dry before you add the water.

Tank cleaning equipment for algae removal (algae magnets, top, and scourers, bottom).

OTHER EQUIPMENT
You will also require the following:
- A siphon or 'hoover' to clean the gravel and change the water (these are sold in aquatic shops),
- A scourer or magnet to clean algae off the inside of the glass (again, found in aquatic shops),
- A clean bucket, with no traces of soap or detergent, for water changes.

Now you have all your aquarium equipment, you should be methodical about setting it up.

When you arrive home with your aquarium, you will probably want to set it up as soon as possible. Unless you are attaching your background with aquarium silicone (see below), you should be able to fill it with water straightaway. However, firstly you need to decide where to position the aquarium. Although you probably already have somewhere in mind, there are a few points to consider.

CHOOSING THE POSITION

Think carefully about positioning, since once the aquarium is filled and in place it cannot be moved without being emptied.

- A glass aquarium filled with gravel, rocks and water is very heavy, and needs to be sited on a sturdy base.
- The floor should also be able to withstand the weight.

Considerable thought should go into the location of your aquarium.

Usually, if the floor will bear an adult human, it will bear an average-sized fish tank, which is, after all, a static weight, but seek advice if you are unsure.

- Position the aquarium near to power points for the sake of convenience, since your filter, heater-thermostat, and lights will all need power. However, the set-up should obviously be positioned so as to avoid the chance of getting the electrical sockets wet when changing water etc. Electrical junction boxes are sold to allow the fishkeeper to wire all the equipment into just one socket, but this does mean you won't usually be able to put a timer on the lighting system.
- There should be convenient access to taps and sinks for water changing.
- Never place the aquarium near a window or too close to radiators, which will affect the tank temperature. Sunlight is also a problem in that it can greatly encourage algae growth. The tank will look much more dramatic in a dark place.
- The fish won't appreciate a position where they are subject to a lot of disturbance, such as many people constantly passing by, or the banging of doors.

STARTING UP

First of all, read any instructions you might have for any or all of the equipment.

- Ensure you have a level surface for your aquarium, and place some polystyrene sheets on top if the tank requires it. Place the tank on top of the sheets.
- Add your background before filling the tank with water. If you are using a background that is stuck inside the aquarium, the silicone glue will usually need 48 hours to dry. Even if you are using a 'picture' stuck on the outside back glass, it's much easier when the tank is empty.
- Rinse the aquarium with tapwater to clean it.
- Rinse the gravel in cold water (e.g. under a running tap) to remove dust, using a clean bucket or a sieve.
- If you are using an undergravel filter in your tank, install it now (with the upright tube connected) on the bottom of the tank.
- Carefully add the gravel. For growing plants use a depth of 5cm (2 inches).
- Half fill the tank with tapwater, then add rocks, wood or ornaments. (You'll disturb the gravel less if you place a saucer on it and pour the water on to that.)
- Always use a water conditioner (also called a dechlorinator), which may be either a tablet or, more usually, a liquid. These are available in aquatic/pet shops, and should be added to any fresh tap water you place in your aquarium, to remove the chlorine disinfectants that are added by the water companies. The disinfectant may be simply chlorine or, less commonly, chloramine. If unsure, choose a dechlorinator that removes both.
- Finish filling the aquarium, then switch on the filter and heater. Never switch on these items if they are not sufficiently submersed.
- Check that everything is working properly.

SETTING UP AN AQUARIUM

① Once you have decided on the tank position, make sure it will be placed on a level surface.

② Place the aquarium on some polystyrene sheets if the tank requires them.

③ Attach the decorative background before filling the tank with water.

④ Wash the gravel in a bucket designated for aquarium use only.

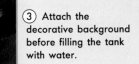

(5) Add the gravel to the tank.

(6) Large décor can then be put into position.

(7) Half-fill the aquarium with water, pouring on to a saucer or into a jug to avoid disturbing the gravel.

(8) Fix the filter and heater-thermostat in place. Then fill the tank with water and switch on the heater-thermostat and filter.

(9) After 24 hours, check the water and adjust the heater-thermostat if necessary.

CHAPTER
3

UNDERSTANDING FILTRATION

Water chemistry can be a complicated subject, but there are a few aspects that a fishkeeper needs to know. Problems with water quality are the most common cause of fish health problems, and should usually be suspected before considering an infectious disease. However, unlike many diseases, water problems are almost totally avoidable if you look after the aquarium properly.

BASIC PRINCIPLES
There are three basic aspects of water quality relevant to keeping fish:
• The water's chemical characteristics – that is to say its pH, its hardness, or its carbonate content.

Your fishes' health is dependent on maintaining good water quality.

- The water's cleanliness – its levels of organic pollution, usually digestive waste matter from the fish.
- Other pollutants – these are usually present in tap water, such as chlorine, and traces of pesticides and heavy metals.

Of these three, by far the most important to the health of the fish is cleanliness. Attributes such as hardness will generally depend on the nature of the domestic tap water in your area, but cleanliness is the job of your filtration system.

CHEMICAL CHARACTERISTICS

pH

Commonly known as acidity or alkalinity, pH is a measure of the water's concentration of hydrogen/hydroxide ions. It is measured on a scale of 0 to 14, 0 being extremely acid, 7 neutral, and 14 extremely alkaline. It is important to remember that the pH scale is logarithmic, meaning that a pH of 7 is 10 times more alkaline than one of 6, and a pH of 8 is 100 times more alkaline.

Fish vary in their pH tolerance and preferences, according to the water conditions from where they originate, but most aquarium fish are happy between pH 6.5 and 8.0.

Remember: never subject fish to sudden pH changes.

The pH level of the aquarium water should be tested regularly.

HARDNESS

This is primarily a measure of the amount of dissolved calcium and magnesium in the water, usually measured in degrees of hardness (dH). Again, fish will vary in their preferences depending on the species, but most can be adapted to your local water hardness conditions. Even if you have very hard water (above 15 degrees on a test kit) you can still keep most types of fish.

It is not easy to attempt water softening. You may wish to arm yourself with water test kits and a book dealing in depth with water quality, such as *Practical Fishkeeping Guide To Filtration and Water Quality* by Dr. Peter Burgess. Your specialist aquatic shop may be able to refer you to other titles. Never use water from domestic softeners or water-softener jugs.

> ### CARBONATE HARDNESS
> Carbonate hardness is a measure of the water's ability to absorb or 'buffer' an acid, due to the quantity of carbonate/bicarbonate ions it contains. Water with a good carbonate hardness (between 4 and 12 degrees) is protected against drops in pH. Again, carbonate hardness will vary depending on your local water supply. Most fish will be happy with this.

WORKING WITH WATER PARAMETERS

Of these water parameters, the most important one for a first-time fishkeeper is pH, since this can drop if you do not change part of your aquarium water for clean water on a frequent enough basis. You can buy simple water test kits yourself, or many aquatic shops offer tests on a sample of your water for a small fee.

With regard to hardness etc., your local dealer will usually be keeping all his/her fish in the local water. If a reputable establishment, they will have acclimatised the fish to the water, and will not keep any that are not happy in it. Do ask your local shop if they adjust their water.

CLEANLINESS AND FILTRATION

As mentioned before, aquarium filters have three functions: mechanical, chemical, biological.

MECHANICAL

The mechanical function collects solid visible waste matter. If you notice your filter flow slowing down, this is the first thing to clean/change. Filter media should be cleaned in the aquarium water to preserve the bacteria if necessary. In the case of an undergravel filter, this may involve 'hoovering' the gravel with a purpose-bought siphon, or discarding filter wool and/or rinsing sponges with other types of filter. However, the filter's more important chemical and biological functions deal with invisible pollutants.

CHEMICAL

This type of filtration is usually carried out by activated carbon, either loose granules in a filter compartment, or occasionally carbon-impregnated sponges. Carbon can

Visible pollution can be removed from the tank by 'hoovering' the substrate with a siphon.

Biological filtration is the most effective way of keeping the aquarium clean, and your fish healthy.

pick up complex substances (such as fish medications or tap-water pesticides), and biological substances (such as fish hormones or the colour from ornamental wood). As such, carbon is useful – but not essential – to have.

The most important thing to bear in mind when using carbon is that the pollutants are merely chemically 'stuck' to it; if it becomes overloaded, the carbon may suddenly and disastrously 'dump' its entire load back into the aquarium water. Therefore it must be changed regularly according to the manufacturer's instructions – usually about once a month. Also, remember always to remove carbon before treating fish with a medication.

Other types of chemical filtration, such as the use of zeolite or peat, are used much more rarely and for different reasons. Interested readers are advised to consult books dealing in water modifications in more depth – ask your specialist aquatic shop for any recommendations.

BIOLOGICAL

This filtration is what really keeps the water clean. Fish naturally release the waste products from digestion and bodily processes straight back into their water. Living in very large lakes or rivers in the wild, this causes no problems as wastes are diluted or flushed away. Living in the confined space of the aquarium, however, these pollutants dissolve in the water, accumulate, and are then breathed in by the fish. Without biological filtration, this would lead to death by poisoning within hours.

Luckily for the fishkeeper, there are types of 'friendly' bacteria that like nothing more than getting a meal by breaking down these pollutants. All these bacteria ask is somewhere to live with a big surface area and a 24-hour flow of well-oxygenated water. This is the function of the biological part of your filter, which may be the gravel bed in an undergravel filter, or sponge or porous rocks in other types of filters.

In the wild, fish waste is diluted naturally in rivers or large lakes. Pictured: Spring-fed Mexican stream.

BIOLOGICAL BREAKDOWN

How does biological breakdown work? The fish release poisonous ammonia into their water as a by-product of digestion. As this is passed through the filter, types of so-called nitrifying bacteria transform it into nitrite – still poisonous, but less so. Other types of nitrifying bacteria then transform the nitrite into nitrate. This is only poisonous at high concentrations, which it should never reach, as it is removed every time you change part of the aquarium water for clean water.

Fish numbers should be increased gradually to avoid a sudden rise in ammonia and nitrite levels.

NEW TANK SYNDROME

Ammonia and nitrite are usually only a problem during the first month or so of a new aquarium, while the bacterial population is establishing itself. During this time, levels of ammonia and nitrite may easily rise high enough to kill fish as there are insufficient bacteria to cope with these poisons. This is known as 'new tank syndrome', and is probably responsible for more fish deaths than any other cause.

The solution is to build up the numbers of fish gradually over two to three months, monitoring ammonia and nitrite levels with water tests as you go. A positive reading of either ammonia or nitrite means the aquarium is not yet ready for any more fish.

If ammonia or nitrite levels are high in spite of your precautions, this is a serious threat to any fish already in the aquarium. Change part of the water (up to a third) for dechlorinated tap water, if necessary on a daily basis, and feed the fish very sparingly until levels come down.

Cultures of nitrifying bacteria are available which can be added to the tank in order to speed up the process. There are also water additives available to render ammonia temporarily less poisonous, although little can be done for nitrite.

FILTER CARE

The biological part of your filter will need maintenance.

- It must run 24 hours a day, or the bacteria will die. This is the main problem with power cuts. Bear in mind that after an hour or so of the filter being turned off, some of the bacteria will have died, and you may experience ammonia and nitrite levels again when the filter re-starts.

- Disturb the biological part of the filter as little as possible. If it is sufficiently blocked to slow down the flow through your filter, you will have to clean it. But only wash part of it at any one time in order to preserve plenty of bacteria. If that is not possible, wash it in water taken from the aquarium rather than

After two to three months, the aquarium water conditions should have stabilised.

tap water, as cold, chlorinated tap water will kill all the bacteria.
• Read the instructions on fish medications. Some of them kill filter bacteria.

Once your aquarium has got past the initial two to three months and is fully stocked, you should not have problems with ammonia or nitrite again, although weekly tests are still advisable.

If positive readings do reappear, you are overstocked, overfeeding, or have done something to kill off your filter bacteria.

WATER CHANGES

Change part of the water for clean dechlorinated tap water on a regular basis. How much and how often will vary from aquarium to aquarium, but 25 per cent per week is a good general guide. This will ensure the pH level stays constant and the nitrate level low (preferably below 50 parts per million as measured on aquarium test kits).

Regular, partial water changes benefit the fish and inhibit algae growth.

If either the pH or nitrate reading of your aquarium water is significantly different to that of your tap water, you are probably not changing enough water. Apart from the benefits to the fish of regular water changes, they will also help to discourage the growth of algae.

AMOUNT TO CHANGE

Don't change more than one-third of the water at any one time (it's too big a physical shock for the fish). Try to match the temperature of the fresh water to that of your aquarium water, and always add a dechlorinator to any water prior to use.

WATER ADDITIVES

Recently, products have come on the market designed to be added to the aquarium weekly, so as to avoid water changes. These principally increase the carbonate hardness in order to keep the pH stable.

However, they do not help much in reducing pollutants and rely on the fishkeeper performing a large

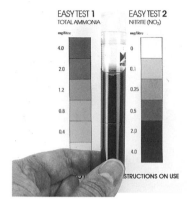

EASY TEST **1**
TOTAL AMMONIA

EASY TEST **2**
NITRITE (NO₂)

mg/litre

4.0

2.0

1.2

0.8

0.4

mg/litre

0

0.1

0.25

0.5

2.0

4.0

STRUCTIONS ON USE

Regular water tests will alert you to any problems in the tank before they become too serious.

water change every six months to compensate. This is not advisable, but these products could be useful every now and then if illness, absence etc. prevents you from doing your usual change. In these situations, they are better than nothing.

WEEKLY TESTS

If your finances permit, test for ammonia, nitrite, nitrate and pH once a week. This would enable you to nip any problems in the bud if they did arise. If this isn't possible, try to keep an eye on at least your nitrate and pH levels with a monthly test. Once a test kit is opened, it must usually be used within six months.

CHAPTER

4

PLANT LIFE

A well-planted aquarium provides a secure environment for the fish.

Most fishkeepers choose to have some live plants, which have both advantages and disadvantages over plastic ones.

ADVANTAGES OF LIVE PLANTS
- Real plants look more natural.
- They may provide food for herbivorous fish.
- They contribute to good water conditions. Specifically, they produce oxygen, and help to remove some of the fish's waste products.
- They should grow and spread if the aquarium conditions suit them.

Natural plants are appreciated by those fish that are mainly
herbivorous, such as the *Otocinclus* catfish, above.

DISADVANTAGES OF LIVE PLANTS
- It can be expensive to buy enough real plants to
  fill an aquarium, particularly if they have to be
  frequently replaced.
- Real plants cannot be cleaned if they accumulate
  algae on their leaves.
- Herbivorous (plant-eating) fish may damage
  them.
- Live plants need regular feeding (usually once a
  week with an aquarium plant food).

Artificial plants
can look very
realistic when
planted, and are
more cost-
effective than
live plants.

CHOOSING PLANTS

Which species of aquatic plants you are able to grow will depend on three factors:

1. The hardness of your water. Most plants dislike hard water, but some species (such as *Cryptocoryne* species) do not mind, and many others will tolerate it.

2. Whether or not you feed them. Plant food is available from most aquatic shops, and will supply the plant with essential trace elements totally lacking in tap water. Aquatic plants need this even more than house plants, as there is no soil in the aquarium. Without a weekly feed, your plants will definitely run out of steam after a while. Liquid foods are better than powders or tablets, as you can adjust the dose more accurately.

3. Most important, though, is the quantity, type and duration of the light you can provide.

Because aquarium plants are not rooted in soil, they need regular feeding.

Cryptocoryne plants usually tolerate hard-water conditions. Pictured: *Crytocoryne nevilli*.

Echinodorus major is a popular aquarium plant that can cope with moderate lighting.

LIGHTING UP

There are many types of fluorescent tubes available for aquariums, but there is a very broad distinction between pinky-coloured lights, which enhance fish coloration, and whiter lights, which favour plant growth. Between these extremes many tubes combine elements of each colour, and most aquarists opt for a compromise.

One factor that does improve your growth and choice of plant life is the possession of twin tubes, since, from a plant's point of view, fluorescent tubes are much less bright than the sun. Similarly, reflectors over the top of your tubes will increase the amount of light reaching the aquarium.

Whatever tube you choose, change it at least once a year, since it will imperceptibly dim with time.

Most fishkeepers switch the light on when they get up in the morning, and off when they go to bed – a period of 16 hours or more. This will not benefit the plants, which require between 10 and 12 hours, and will encourage algae. Fitting a timer is a good idea.

Readers truly interested in aquatic plants are advised to consult a book dealing specifically in the subject, but listed below are some of the types more commonly found for sale in aquatic shops. Although the majority do better in softer water, they will tolerate most waters.

PLANTING THE TANK
Plants suited to single-tube lighting

Indian fern (*Ceratopteris sp.*).

Hygrophila polysperma.

Vallisneria sp.

Java fern (*Microsorium pteropus*).

PLANTS SUITED TO ONE TUBE LIGHT INCLUDE:

African fern (*Bolbitis heudelotii*)

Amazon swords (most *Echinodorus* species)

Ambulia (*Limnophila sessiliflora*)

Anubias **species**

Crypts (*Cryptocoryne* species)

Elodea (*Egeria densa*)

'Giant' hygrophila (*Hygrophila corymbosa 'stricta'*)

Hygrophila (*Hygrophila polysperma*)

Indian ferns (*Ceratopteris cornuta, Ceratopteris thalictroides*)

Java fern (*Microsorium pteropus* and assorted cultivars)

Java moss (*Vesicularia dubyana*)

Onion plants (*Crinum* species)

Vallis (*Vallisneria* species).

A well-planted tank is especially important in a community aquarium, where fish require the security of cover. Pictured: characins and catfish.

PLANTS SUITED TO TWIN-LIGHTING INCLUDE:
Those plants suited to one tube light (see opposite), although species such as *Anubias* may pick up algae in a brighter aquarium.
Alternanthera species
Most *Aponogeton* species
Bacopa species
Cabomba (*Cabomba caroliniana*)
Hydrocotyle species
Ludwigia (*Ludwigia glandulosa*, *Ludwigia repens*)
Wisteria (*Hygrophila difformis*).

Whether a particular plant thrives in the aquarium seems to vary from fishkeeper to fishkeeper, sometimes for no apparent reason. Seek advice from aquatic shop staff, who should be acquainted with local water conditions, and remember that an aquarium is not a natural home for some types of aquatic plant. However, with good light and weekly feeding, you should achieve a pleasant effect.

Some plants require double-tube lighting. Pictured: *Ludwigia* sp.

Water wisteria (*Hygrophila difformis*) also requires double-tube lighting.

CHAPTER
5

SELECTING TROPICAL FISH

When choosing your first fish, you are at the mercy of your aquatic retail outlet. Unless you trust them to give you truthful and accurate answers to queries on a fish's eventual size, feeding habits etc., you will have to arm yourself with a fish encyclopaedia or a knowledgeable friend. Obviously, though, finding a good shop is a better idea, as experienced retail staff will often have more practical knowledge than either your friend or your encyclopaedia.

A happy community aquarium is reliant on the fishkeeper successfully mixing and matching the right tankmates.

Some fish, including some Lake Victoria cichlid species, require caves so they can hide in the event of danger.

IMPORTANT CONSIDERATIONS

There are a number of factors to consider before buying your fish:

- Will it be happy in my water?
- Will it be happy at my temperature?
- How tolerant is it of ammonia/nitrite/nitrate levels? (Especially if your aquarium is newly set up.)
- What size will it eventually reach?
- Is my tank roomy enough for its swimming habits?
- How long is it likely to live?
- What does it like to feed on?
- Does it feed on the bottom or on the surface?
- Does it need to feed during the day or in the dark?
- Does it need others of its own kind to be happy, or does it display aggression towards its own kind?

- Should it be kept only with other males/females of the same kind, and how many of each?
- Does it damage plants?
- Does it hide all the time or some of the time?
- Does it need a cave, a hiding place, or the presence of plants to feel secure?
- Finally, is it compatible with my other fish?

COMPATIBLE SPECIES

This is the area where retail staff are likely to be most useful. However, here are a few broad guidelines to compatibility that apply to all fish:

- Don't put predatory fish with others small enough to be eaten. However, if the fish are too large to be swallowed, most predators will not bother them.

Very predatory fish, such as the Piranha, *Pygocentrus nattereri* (pictured), should only be placed with their own kind.

Long-finned species, such as the Angel fish (left), should never be housed with fin-nippers. Discus (right) are respectful of their tankmates' body parts.

- Long-finned fish should not be kept with species that tend to nip fins.
- Don't put fast feeders with slow feeders – the slow feeders will starve.
- Don't put fast-moving fish with slow-moving, nervous ones – the nervous ones will be perpetually stressed and frightened.
- If you are keeping fish that need a hiding place, make sure you provide enough caves for them all.
- When stocking a new aquarium, add the most peaceful fish first, and the most aggressive last.
- Bear in mind that fish of different species may start off the same size but end up very different. However, larger fish that have grown up all their lives with smaller ones often fail to see them as dinner even when they have now become bite-sized!

Fish that display social behaviour, such as these Two-spot Barbs, should be kept in groups.

- Keep fish that exhibit social behaviour in groups of three or more. This will prevent the bullying that can occur when there are just two individuals. Similarly, fish with a tendency to harass other species are often no trouble if they have plenty of their own kind with which to interact.
- Generally speaking, the larger your aquarium, the less likely you are to experience conflicts.

COMMUNITY FISH

Many shops advertise certain species as 'community' fish. This can be a useful guide to those types which tend to be easier to keep and give few aggression problems. It does not automatically mean you can keep all 'community' fish together, though.

STOCKING LEVEL

When considering the overall stocking level of your aquarium, it is the amount of inches of fish body that count, rather than the number of individuals. A general rule is 1 inch (2.5 cm) per gallon, then increase to 2 inches (5 cm) after 6 months.

However, the capacity of your filtration system really counts more than the surface area of your aquarium, and this can be difficult to judge. With the above rule as a guide, use test kits. If you have ammonia/nitrite problems after three months or have trouble keeping your nitrate levels down, you are probably overstocked. Remember to stock a new tank gradually.

INTRODUCING FISH

The shop will pack your fish in plastic bags and cover them with something to protect them from the light – being exposed to light while already very frightened is extremely stressful to fish. For the same reason, turn off your aquarium light before you begin to unpack them. Float the sealed bags on the surface of the aquarium water for 20-30 minutes, in order to allow the temperatures of the two to equalise.

Introduce the fish to the tank with great care to avoid unnecessary stress.

Float the sealed bags on the surface of the aquarium water to acclimatise the fish to the temperature.

Then simply cut the bags open and gently pour the fish into the tank water. Leave the lights off for at least an hour, or until the next morning, even if this means your resident fish will miss a meal (most fish will not feed properly in the dark or semi-dark, apart from nocturnal species – see Chapter Six).

It is often said that you should not add the water in which the fish have been travelling in to your aquarium, as it is a small amount and likely to be badly polluted. This would be true if the fish had been in it for hours, but this is rarely the case, and netting the fish out of the bag will greatly increase its stress levels.

After 20–30 minutes, release the fish into the tank.

Similarly it is frequently suggested that the fishkeeper opens the bag every five minutes or so and mixes a small amount of aquarium water with the fish's own water, in order to acclimatise the fish to the water conditions in the tank. This is not a good idea. Firstly, you should not be adding a fish to your aquarium that has come from water with very different chemical characteristics to yours. Secondly, no effective physical acclimatisation can occur in 20 minutes anyway (this would take at least 24 hours, usually more). And thirdly this will greatly increase the stress the fish experiences.

Keep a close check on your fish to ensure that species are truly compatible.

If you do encounter problems with a fish's size or compatibility after you have bought it, the shop may take it back. But since compatibility problems are unpredictable and you probably knew its eventual size before you bought it, its ultimate welfare is your responsibility. It is not acceptable to kill an animal simply for growing too large or for following its natural instincts. If you do want to return something, discuss this with the shop first, don't just turn up with a dripping bag!

CHAPTER 6

THE RIGHT DIET

Many people are surprised to find that aquarium fish need feeding almost as often as us humans. Almost all of the species commonly kept in home aquariums need two to three small meals a day. The exception to this would be genuine predatory species (those which, in the wild, would normally eat other fish) who may need feeding only once a day or even every few days. For obvious reasons though, these species are less usually kept.

Because of work commitments, most fishkeepers can only feed twice a day, but don't get into the habit of feeding less often than this – fish can't thrive on one meal a day any more than you could.

Most tropical fish species require two to three small meals per day.

Good-quality flake food should form the basis of the fish's diet.

BASIC RULES

- Feed two to three times a day, no more than can be consumed in five minutes. Overfeeding causes water problems, overweight fish, and clogs filters. Don't simply go for a 'pinch' – this means different amounts to different people. If you have overfed, try to remove the excess by siphoning it out.
- Allow the fish at least 10 minutes to 'wake up' in the morning after you have switched the light on before you offer them food.
- Make a good-quality complete dry food (flake or pellets) the basis of the fish's diet. These foods contain all the necessary essential nutrients.
- Use common sense and tailor the food particle size to the size of your fish's mouths. If you are keeping small fish, say, less than 5 cms (2 ins) long, use either flake or the so-called 'micro pellets'. Sometimes,

Larger fish species require pellet food.

Bottom-feeders 'hoover' up any food missed by the other fish. Pictured: red-tailed black shark (*Epalzeorhynchos bicolor*).

individual flakes can be quite large though, and may need crumbling between your fingers before use.

- If you have larger fish, you will probably find pellets cleaner and easier to feed than flakes. Choose a pellet that is aimed at the type of fish you are keeping, for example a general pellet or a cichlid pellet.

- Fish that feed off the bottom of the tank can be quite useful in 'hoovering up' any food that the upper feeders miss. But never expect them to get by just on this – your surface-feeders may not miss any food, and almost certainly won't miss enough for the bottom-feeders to survive. Special foods that sink immediately can be bought, which usually look like tablets or chocolate buttons. These are nibbled and are exceptions to the usual 'five-minute rule'; they should be eaten within two hours.

Bottom-feeders should be fed fast-sinking food, such as algae wafers.

- Some fish may need to feed at twilight or during the night. These are usually the catfish types, and will be happy with a sinking tablet dropped in five minutes after lights out.
- The best people to ask about feeding are the retail staff who sell you the fish. They will usually know not only what the fish needs to eat, but also what it is used to eating in the shop.
- Feeding-time is the best time to observe your fish for compatibility problems or first signs of illness.
- Keep fish food in a cool, dry place, and, once opened, use it up within three months.

LIVE FOOD

Fish health does seem to benefit from natural foods such as bloodworms, mosquito larvae, brine shrimp etc. (although no one is quite sure why). Feed these no more than once a day, preferably after they have had a small amount of dried food. Fish love natural foods and will devour them if given the chance. Feeding solely these can be unhealthy, as these foods are not as nutritionally balanced as prepared foods.

It is not a good idea to feed certain live foods (such as *Tubifex* worms) when they are actually alive, because of the risk of disease transmission. Instead, they are available frozen (but defrost them before use),

'Live' food, such as bloodworms, glassworms, brine shrimps, and Daphnia, can transmit disease. Instead, these foods can be bought frozen and irradiated (top) and freeze–dried (bottom).

freeze-dried, or, recently, preserved in jelly form in packets. Most fishkeepers find fish accept frozen or packaged 'live' foods more readily than freeze-dried ones, although the latter are cheaper. Enquire whether the fish has any special needs for natural foods before you buy it.

SUPPLEMENTING THE DIET

You can supplement your fish's diet with other things if you wish. Fishkeepers often give herbivore fish some lettuce, cucumber, courgettes and blanched spinach or peas. Carnivores can be given pieces of fish or prawns. Just bear in mind the following:

A lettuce can be given as an occasional treat to herbivorous fish.

- High-protein foods, such as prawns, could cause pollution if left in the aquarium. Net or siphon them out after a couple of hours.
- Although fish need unsaturated fats (found in plants, fish and shellfish), they are not adapted to deal with saturated fats (found in dairy products, eggs and meat) – don't feed these foods.
- Always use a prepared food like flake or pellets as the basic diet. Don't rely totally on cucumber, prawns etc.

CHAPTER 7

HEALTH MATTERS

Water quality is the most frequent cause of fish health problems, but infectious diseases obviously do occur. Fish medicine is almost as complicated as human medicine, and there is only room here for some general guidelines. Again, a trustworthy retail outlet is probably your best friend, if available.

Some fish diseases may need veterinary-prescribed drugs, but it can be very difficult to locate a vet with any fish knowledge. If you do need one, ask your own vet for any recommendations.

Observe your fish closely for a few minutes every day to spot any unusual behaviour or early signs of ill health.

Clamped fins can indicate a health problem.

SPOTTING A SICK FISH

Apart from the obvious symptoms of illness (spots, wounds etc.), a sick fish will also exhibit general signs of distress. These will often be the first thing you notice.

- A darker or paler colour than usual
- Fins may be 'clamped' instead of erect
- Breathing may be heavy and/or rapid
- Refusal to feed
- Loss of weight/not putting on weight as expected
- Scratching on aquarium ornaments
- Darting unusually rapidly around the aquarium
- Resting at the water surface/on the bottom (if not normal behaviour)
- Hiding (if not normal behaviour).

WATER PROBLEMS

If you experience fish health problems, do a water test before anything else. Test for ammonia, nitrite, nitrate, pH, and check the aquarium temperature. Don't assume there is not an environmental cause simply because only one fish is affected – individuals even of the same species vary in their tolerance.

If your water is acceptable but showing some problems, it may have been bad when the fish began to fall ill. Even if the water condition has since improved,

If you encounter problems, carry out a water test. Poor-quality water is often responsible for fish sickness.

it could still have been the cause. Your water does not necessarily have to be bad to cause a fish illness, just different either from what it requires, or what it is used to. Even where there is clearly an infectious disease, poor water quality may be a contributory factor by weakening the fish's immune system.

SOCIAL CAUSES

If you have ruled out water quality and temperature, also consider:

A change in a fish's behaviour is not always health-related — social and environmental causes are common.

- Is the fish being repeatedly bullied?
- Is it engaged in sexual behaviour?
- Is it simply suffering from old age?
- Is it nervous because it lacks others of its own kind to shoal with?
- Is it stressed from being recently moved?
- Does it lack a suitable home or hiding place?
- Are you feeding it the correct food, in the correct amount, at the correct frequency?

Even if the fish has an obvious infectious disease, consider if any of the above problems may have weakened it and so rendered it vulnerable.

QUARANTINE
Many diseases can be avoided by the fishkeeper using a quarantine aquarium. This is a separate, empty tank where new arrivals or sick fish can be kept in isolation for two to six weeks. Unfortunately, perhaps for financial reasons, very few fishkeepers bother with this.

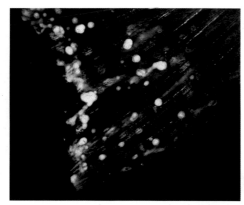

Ichthyophthirius (white spot) is a common problem in aquaria. Here is a close-up of numerous white spots on a fish's fin.

COMMON DISEASES

The most common fish diseases are shown in the table (below). If you can't find your symptoms here, or the treatments suggested are not working, consult either a vet or a fish-health consultant, a book dealing with a wider range of fish health problems, or your local aquarist shop – preferably all three.

POSSIBLE SIGNS OF INFECTIOUS DISEASE

The scientific names of some disease-causing organisms are given below. This information may assist when selecting suitable treatments.

SYMPTOMS	POSSIBLE CAUSES (IN ORDER OF PROBABILITY)	TREATMENT
Small white spots over the fish's body and fins.	① Spots less than 1 mm in size: Whitespot parasites (*Ichthyophthirius*). ② Some spots much larger than 1 mm and typically in clusters: Viral Disease (*Lymphocystis*).	① A shop-bought whitespot remedy. If the condition does not improve, you may have a different parasite. Try a copper sulphate-based remedy. ② No available treatment. However, the fish usually eventually recover by themselves.
Heavy, rapid breathing, without other symptoms.	Gill parasites.	Shop-bought treatment aimed at treating parasites.

White patches on the fish's mouth or body.	① 'Mouth fungus'; a bacterial infection (*Flexibacter* species). Progresses rapidly to death within 24-36 hours.	① Vet-prescribed antibiotics. Remove or destroy any affected fish.
	② Neon Tetra Disease. Internal infection of some tetras and, less commonly, some danios and barbs. Appears as white bands on the body. Slow; not very infectious.	② No effective treatment. Remove or destroy affected fish.
	③ Guppy disease. Affects guppies and some other livebearers. Rare, often fatal, but slow.	③ Shop-bought copper sulphate-based treatment.
Ragged, blood-streaked fins.	① Physical damage from a tank-mate.	① Remove the bully or the victim.
	② Fin rot. A bacterial infection from injury, poor water or severe whitespot infection.	② Shop-bought fin rot treatment; if very advanced, use vet-prescribed antibiotics.
Cloudy eyes	If only one eye is affected, physical injury is the likely cause. If both, poor water quality.	Improve the water or consider how the fish injured itself.

Scratching on ornaments, swimming rapidly on the spot, breathing quickly, having a grey, slimy look to the skin.	Single-celled parasites on the skin and/or gills.	Shop-bought remedy aimed at 'slime and velvet disease'.
Pop-eye (eye sticking out).	If only one eye is affected, a local infection. If both eyes, see below.	Shop-bought bacterial treatment.
Pop-eye in both eyes, panting, dropsy (a marked swelling of the fish's abdominal area, to the extent that the scales stick out), a blood-streaked abdomen.	A systemic infection (a general infection of the fish's whole body), usually bacterial in origin. Recovery is unlikely, but treat the aquarium to protect the other inhabitants.	Preferably vet-prescribed antibiotics, otherwise shop-remedies aimed at 'internal bacterial infections'.
Ulcers (open sores), extreme weight loss.	A similar systemic infection to pop-eye, panting, dropsy (see above). Associated with a slow progress of the disease.	As for Pop-eye (above).
Fluffy yellow-white or grey growths.	Fungus. Secondary infection following physical damage or stress (e.g. from poor water quality, bullying, or a previous infection).	Easily cured with a shop-bought fungus treatment, but you must address the original cause.

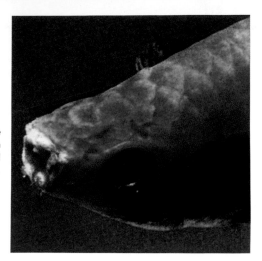

Fungus on the damaged mouth of a poeciliid livebearer.

IMPORTANT POINTS
- Because fish cannot tell you when they feel unwell, you will lose the occasional fish for no apparent reason. This is normal, and at least in your aquarium they do not have to worry about finding food or avoiding predators when feeling ill.
- Only worry about losing your fish if you have definite signs of infectious disease in your aquarium, or you are losing more than the occasional fish.
- None of the common aquarium fish diseases are thought seriously to affect humans, but it is still a good idea to wash your hands thoroughly after they have been in the aquarium. As a precautionary measure, always avoid immersing open cuts in the aquarium water.
- Most importantly, please don't let the above list of diseases frighten you. If you buy quarantined fish from a recommended retail outlet and look after them properly, you will very rarely experience infectious disease problems.

USING MEDICATIONS

- Don't use medications as a purely preventative measure. Over-use of any treatment is harmful to the health of fish and plants, and encourages the organisms that cause disease to become drug-resistant.
- Never exceed the manufacturer's recommended dose.
- If you have carbon in your filter, remove it before using a medication.
- Read all the instructions on the bottle before use.
- Some (though not many) treatments kill filter bacteria – these will say so on the bottle.
- Many treatments cannot be used with invertebrates such as crabs, shrimps and snails (read the instructions). If you have these, you will have to re-house them somewhere for the duration.
- Some treatments lower oxygen levels. Make sure the aquarium has either air from an air pump or plenty of surface movement from your filter outlet.

If you take care when buying your fish, and maintain a clean, healthy aquarium you should rarely encounter disease in your fish.

- When you have finished using a treatment, perform at least a 25 per cent water change. If you need to re-treat, follow the instructions on the bottle.
- Avoid inhaling chemical treatments or spilling them on your skin.

EUTHANASIA

If you have to kill a fish, the acceptable method is to remove it from the aquarium, hold it firmly in something like a towel, and hit it hard and quickly on the head (with a hammer or suchlike), in such a way as to totally destroy its brain. If you feel unable to do this, you will have to get a vet to administer a lethal dose of anaesthetic.

There are no other methods considered humane. The important thing is to spare the fish from suffering, not yourself.

CHAPTER
8

APPENDIX

DAILY CHECKS

① Feed the fish 2 (or 3) times per day – once in the morning and once in the evening.

② Check the water temperature reading on your thermometer.

③ Check that your filter and other equipment is running properly.

④ Check for any fish that are unwell.

WEEKLY CHECKS

① Change 25 per cent of the aquarium water for clean water of approximately the same temperature. Don't forget to add a dechlorinator to the new water.

② Clean your filter, if necessary.

③ Hoover the gravel, if necessary.

④ Wipe the inside front of the aquarium (and the sides if you wish) to remove algae.

⑤ Prune your plants to remove surplus or scruffy leaves, and add your plant food.

⑥ Check your water for ammonia, nitrite, nitrate and pH.

DID YOU KNOW?

■ Practical Fishkeeping is Britain's best-selling fishkeeping magazine
■ Practical Fishkeeping is published four weekly.
■ It covers every area of the hobby for every fishkeeper from newcomer to expert.
■ It covers tropical freshwater fish from community species to the rare and unusual and marine tropical fish and inverts.
■ We look at ponds of all shapes and sizes from goldfish to Koi - coldwater aquarium fish.
■ We publish hard-edged, in depth, up to date reviews of all the equipment you need to run a successful aquarium or pond.
■ If you want to know more about the great hobby of fishkeeping it's exactly what you need

Practical Fishkeeping
Introductory subscription offer

To subscribe to Practical Fishkeeping magazine, simply call

0845 601 1356

and quote FB11/A67 to receive 6 issues at a special price. Offer only open to UK residents.
For details of overseas rates, please call **+44 (0)1858 468811.**

Practical Fishkeeping, Bretton Court, Bretton, Peterborough PE3 8DZ, Great Britain Tel: 01733 282764